BLOOD SUGAR CANTO

BLOOD SUGAR CANTO

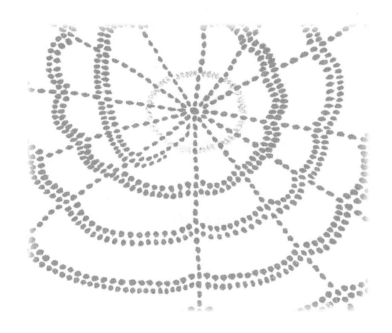

ire'ne lara silva

SADDLE ROAD PRESS

Saddle Road Press
Hilo, Hawai'i
www.saddleroadpress.com

Cover art by Moisés S. L. Lara
Cover and book design by Don Mitchell

ISBN 978-0991395286
Library of Congress Control Number: 2015954081

for everyone with diabetes
and everyone who loves them
may each of you find your own best path

CONTENTS

v.   *let my last breath be song*

i. speak with your voice touch with my hands

you do not listen

you do not listen in broad daylight alone amongst others
you do not listen i fight surrendering to you i fight fighting
you i fight what you have given me and what you have not
you take away as much as you give allowing me to foresee
the peace beyond mourning beyond loss beyond grieving i
cannot wrestle you cannot defeat you why must i look to
you when i am alone and when i am afraid and when i am
lost

>   you are a river of rage—you—many-headed and
>   many-limbed you are the chaos of ecstasy and the
>   hurt of blood seeping through borders—you are not
>   just you are not mercy you have given me loss you
>   have given me loss you have given me loss   you
>   have   given   me
>   loss

some mornings i do not want to live you send me yellow-
winged butterflies some mornings i do not want to speak
you send me the wind some mornings i do not want to fight
you send me machetes fitted to my hands some days i do not
want to grieve you send me love i cannot refuse

>   you have brought me song when i have raged you
>   have brought me song when i have hurt you have
>   brought me song when i have loved you have made
>   me song you have made me song and made me sing
>   to a broken broken life a beautiful world a broken
>   broken world a beautiful life

i cannot breathe anymore   life i cannot sigh anymore
       life everywhere on the road there are roses and
everywhere there is clamor and you will not hear me
       life when i whisper thank you

april 23, 2008

i kept putting off my doctor's
appointment what didn't i want to
hear my brother pushed me to go i
don't know would i have waited
until i was in the hospital i don't
remember was it cool was it sunny i
drove myself there i drove myself
away

diabetes mellitus she said knowingly
nodding her head i don't remember
what she said afterwards i was a
grown woman no weeping no one to
hold my hand no curling into a ball i
had to at least pretend to listen
while she put the glucose monitor in
my hand and the sample kit of
lancets and testing strips *this is to
get you started* while she gave me
sample insulin pens with i forget
three or five sample needle pen tips
and told me *10 units a day to begin
with* and she showed me how to
assemble it and where i should
inject it *belly thighs upper arms* i
think i nodded i said yes i
understood i said thank you

i remember she asked me what i
needed the only thing i could think
to ask for was time i needed time
away from work i needed time to

think i couldn't work twelve hour
days and worry about quotas and
concentrate while i spoke on the
phone and sent emails and turned in
paperwork i couldn't i couldn't

i drove home i don't remember
driving home it wasn't that far it
could have been a million miles i
looked no different no one could see
it the diabetes on me inside me no
bleeding wound the doctor didn't
say you have this long to live i could
walk and talk and think and go on
but i felt broken i felt like there was
no reason to go on i wanted to say
no i can't do this i can't live this
i wanted to die i was afraid

song for fear

i think you live in my blood
running always running
living in my belly
living in my blood
living in my eyes

i have been searching for you
wanted to know where
you lived in my body
so that i could uproot you
set you on fire smoke you out
lance you drain you
bleed you render you nothing
less than nothing

but here you have been
cradled against me
a changeling child
racing in my blood
terrorizing my organs
draining my strength
leaving me alone in
a world of narrow bridges

when i was a child
i was afraid of the
roaring lion in the hallway
afraid of cockroaches
afraid of my father's anger

i am afraid of other things now
my body out of control
exhaustion

amputation
dying before my brother
and leaving him defenseless

i am afraid of more losses
that will call me to be
stronger than i am

i see you now
fear
there is a place for you here
and there is work for you
but you cannot remain
rampant and uncontrolled
you cannot claim
my entire body as your
refuge your hideout your food

in return
i promise
not to eat you

i won't tear at you
with my teeth
poisoning myself
i will watch over you
and it will be safe
for you to be a small
and furred creature
and at dawn i will remember
to sing to you too

there are many roads
and the sun and the rain
and the wind and the earth
will give us shelter
we do not have to be afraid

despair, you are invited to my table

you may sit here and eat with me
it is a simple table   there are no utensils
i made this food   i poured this water
i watched these beans   simmer for hours
the corn tortillas   i made by hand

you have my eyes   you have my mouth
we have my face   we have my hands
we fold our corn tortillas the same way
if i wasn't speaking   if you weren't cursing
we would be   mirror reflections
i speak with your voice   you touch with my hands

it had never occurred to me   to invite you here
i was so busy fighting you   declaring that you didn't exist
i thought everyone   lived this way   with their despair
hiding you until both your name and my name
lost all meaning   all distinction

what can live there   in that place   where you are everything
despair,   i want to live
let us find a way to live peacefully with our same face
no more battles   no more wounded
live in me   i will live in you

you have taught me what no one else could
let me be the one who learned to live with you
we have stories to tell each other
sit here and eat with me

diabetic love song

understand there are things i will never do with you
i will never go to the beach with you in the summer
i will never share a stack of pancakes with you
i will never stay up all night
tossing back tequila shots or beers
i need naps and i need rest
and when i get too tired i stop functioning
my brain begins its meltdown at 90 degrees
i will cancel plans
this will all be more than i can bear

and now there are pills in the morning
and pills at night and more than one syringe a day
there may be three there may be four
and everywhere everywhere there are alcohol pads
in the house in the restroom on the floor in my purse in my pocket
and spent lancets and testing strips with one miniscule drop of blood
and i will always be pricking my fingers and pricking my fingers
and pricking pricking pricking

i can never skip meals
i will always need more water
i will always have doctors' appointments looming
and sometimes i will rail against all of it
howl and gnash my teeth and throw things about
i will despair and there will be nothing you can do
and sometimes when i am tired and hungry
i will become a screaming monster
felled only by exhaustion

given that time is short
given that the number of my days is unknown
i have no patience now for people who put off their dreams

people without dreams
people dedicated to accumulation and consumption
people who fill their lives with drama and noise
because they can think of nothing better to do
given that time is short
i will cut corners everywhere
and preserve energy for what is essential:
creating and passion and love and beauty and quiet
i will never make beds or iron or clean baseboards
will never go to a mall or a baby shower
or any event for the sake of appearances
i will never again try to make my family love me

                                    i will always be
                     working on letting go of things that hurt me
                    will always be intent on healing on becoming stronger
                      and sometimes that will make me flint-faced and harsh
                    and sometimes it will make me the compassionate being
                                    i want to live my life as
                       and sometimes i won't know the difference

but if you stay
if you stay
i will love you always
love you fiercely
love you as if you were the only one i ever loved
love you like my last hope

                                          my only hope
                       i will give you the light of my eyes
                             and the touch of my lips
                             and the hot of my hands
                             i will be your road going

and your road returning
and most of all
most of all
i promise
i will never give up

dieta indigena

what would we be if we were still
what our ancestors ate
there were no cows no pigs no chickens here
there were no domesticated animals
animals fattened beyond their ability
to survive in the wild
bred to feeble-mindedness

there were javelinas serpents turtles fish pheasants
and further north buffalo moose deer
none of them raised in captivity misery
none of them pumped with hormones
no Oestradiol Progesterone Testosterone
no Zeranol Trenbolone Melengestrol
no meat injected with ammonia dioxin
no cloned meat no poisoned meat

500 years and our bodies
cannot adjust to this foreign diet
and not just we but all humans
cannot thrive on a diet of chemicals
and preservatives
sulfur dioxide sodium benzoate sodium nitrate
propyl gallate BHA BHT
food prepared food poisoned with
partially hydrogenated oils trans fats saturated fats

and what have they done to maíz
our first food
the corporations have created maíz
which bears no viable seed
they would have us eating maíz
born infertile born artificial born dead

what is a food that is not fertile
we are the eaters of fruit and seed
the eaters of that which has eaten fruit and seed
sustenance of fertility of blooming of gestating
our lives fed by what is alive

but if we listen to the ancestors
there is still food we can eat
food which can renew our health
food we can grow with our own hands
food which has grown in fields close to us
chiles frijoles tomates aguacate calabaza
nopales chayote cacao amaranth quinoa
food we should eat
food we must eat
sustenance our bodies have craved
all these centuries
let us eat what our ancestors ate
decolonize your diet *mi raza*
it is time to regain our strength

ii.   read the ache of telling so much truth

poem to frida, patron saint of art and pain

half my life frida   half my life has passed since i first
saw your paintings   the photographs of you   your
magnificent eyes   pools of fury and pain   shooting
sparks and light-swallowing tenderness   the lines
bracketing your mouth scoring your eyes   the line of
your lips which read the ache of telling so much truth
the ache of your defiant silence you would not weep
your body's pain in anything but paint *what do i need
feet for if i have wings* you said   and cast your physical
body   into   the   sky

          i am not as strong as you frida   i am not as
brave   when i am in pain i want to cry   i want to give
up i want someone to hold me someone to carry me   i
want to not have a body   half my life ago i could
admire you laying in bed   your torso in a cast
flowers in your hair i kept tiny postcard prints of **the
broken column** and **the wounded deer**   and
worshipped the tears from your eyes poetry for my eyes
speaking   the   weeping   in   my   heart

                    but what did i know
girl that i was who had never known pain without
escape who had never known loss without remedy   girl
that i was who still dreamed with innocent fervor   who
did not know how to fear   it is true as you said *we can
endure much more than we think we can*   but now i see
your wounds in **the tree of hope remain strong**   and
the disintegrating woman   in **the circle**   and i want
to fall down weeping for you   you hurt   you hurt so
much and no amount of gold dust could ever hide the
blood you shed   the tears you shed   i want to protect
you from those who would render you a metaphor

when you were a flesh and blood
woman frida   an artist who lived so ferociously your
work your words   have burned into so many of us
and you said *i am not sick i am broken but i am happy as
long as i can paint*   and what more do we need to
continue our art when we are afraid   when we are
tired   when we are alone when we are in pain   *ay*
frida   may my little poems burn like embers and rise
like crimson smoke   like tattered phoenixes in your
memory   and in honor of those for whom each step is
an effort   an agony   an internal blaze of lightning
scorching muscle and bone

"we don't give morphine for heartburn"

doctor dossantos, you would have left my brother to die
you saw him, a young brown-skinned man with scars and tattoos

and decided after a five second examination to discharge him
"we don't give morphine for heartburn," you said and turned away

when we returned to the emergency room a few days later
the doctor read your notes and turned us away within minutes

and the next three doctors did the same and every time the nurses too
were more calloused and wouldn't listen though i pleaded and pleaded

doctor, you left us desperate, him writhing in pain, me helpless and
unable to help, i watched him grow sicker, turn yellow, and when it
was more than he could bear

we readied ourselves again for the drive to the only hospital that took
patients without insurance, readied ourselves for the hours-long
wait to see a doctor

finally there was one who realized what was going on and within a
few minutes had him admitted and before the sun rose, he was

scheduled for surgery later that afternoon and for the first time
in days, i saw his pain ease when they started the morphine drip

there was so much to learn, so much to accept, not just this needed
surgery but to learn he was diabetic and had high blood pressure
and high cholesterol

many doctors after that and for several days i slept on the floor
of that hospital room and finally, though he was weak

and recovering, with a new eleven-inch wound, he was no longer
nauseous and in pain and in need of help i could not give him

i am grateful for that, every day i am grateful i didn't lose him
i am grateful that we went back and went back and insisted and insisted

but doctor dossantos, I curse your name, every time I pass that hospital
every time I think of you, I hope, one day, you are left writhing waiting

mad with pain, I hope you are ignored, dismissed, left helpless
I cannot forgive you, doctor, I will never forgive you, I hope you burn
in hell.

diabetic epidemic

la azucar we heard it whispered first
la azucar they said but it made no sense
the sugar the sugar she died from *la azucar*
at first it was only the old people
the only difference we saw
was that coffee needed sweet'n low instead of sugar
and maybe they'd eat only half a piece of *pan dulce*
instead of two

and then it was my father
i was ten he seemed the same
nothing we could see was different
though every morning he pulled out a vial
from the refrigerator and gave himself a shot
they told him he had to eat differently
but didn't tell him why or how to eat the food
in the little guidebook
half of which he'd never seen before

and there were stories but those were about other people
years passed and then it was everyone's grandparents
and some aunts and uncles though they were all at least fifty years old
we heard of children who had it but only saw them on tv with jane
fonda while on mexican tv there were all these commercials that said
this pill this plant this doctor can make you better

la azucar was everywhere
but not as scary as cancer cancer would kill you
i went to college and learned nothing at all about it
and then returned to south texas
where the people are ninety eight percent
hispanic latino mexican tejano whatever name they like most
and by this time people could say *la azucar* and everyone understood

not to insist not another tortilla no more cake no beer
and there was splenda and diet coke and sugar free snow cones
in every restaurant and on every corner

everything changed when it was my brother my youngest brother
in the hospital for gallstones though it took two weeks, six e.r. visits
and two hospital admittances before they operated
and it was on the third or fourth visit when they asked
did you know you're diabetic
and said *oh and you have high blood pressure and high cholesterol*
and are you a pima indian I've read studies many pima indians
have all three diabetes high blood pressure and high cholesterol

everything i learned from my brother i shared
with anyone who asked anyone who confided in me
how many people on the verge of tears who didn't understand why
old people young people thin people
round people white people brown people
everyone says type two diabetes can be controlled with diet and exercise
they lay all the blame on obesity but not everybody is the same
there are all kinds of factors all kinds of resistances
and the right medication for one person is wrong for another

i changed my diet gave up drinking
thought i'd managed not to become a target
no one told me not sleeping and skipping meals and stress
and living on adrenaline could tear the body down
or that insulin resistance was part of polycystic ovarian syndrome
and then that day came the confirmation from the doctor
and my first shot of insulin and now *la azucar* was in my body
part of my life and it was a while
before i could see anything outside myself
without my brother i think i would have given up given in

it took awhile but then i opened my eyes
and noticed that *la azucar* was all around me
the woman next to me at work
the early morning bus driver
every third person at my other job
and the man at the store puzzling over egg substitutes
and the waitress downing a shot of orange juice during a long shift
and everywhere i see the warning signs in people's behaviors
in their complaints symptoms beyond passing
thirst or temporary blood sugar lows
but no one listens
why isn't there screaming in the streets
the children are diabetic the pregnant women are diabetic
so many people of color so many poor and working class
and the food is making us sick
and every day there are more and more of us
and *la azucar* is claiming lives and limbs and whole families
why is *la azucar* still being whispered
we should be screaming it

labwork

i gave them
my arm i've found it hurts less
if i watch everything but the exact
moment the needle pierces my vein my
blood is a deep almost black red i watch it
being drawn
out of me enough to fill three vials

i remember when my blood was bright
red the red of poinsettias the red
of other people's blood

it's not my imagination, i said to the
young nurse, my blood is darker than it
was, isn't it... yes, she said, flicking her
ponytail,
it's the insulin

of all the changes diabetes has brought to
my body the sensitivity to heat the
painfully dry skin the weight gain the
exhaustion
this change in the color of my blood
makes me sad seems to say i am changed

changed irredeemably
changed without return

what else of me has changed
what would i tell the lover now the one
who said my skin carried the scent of
sunlight and maíz the one who murmured
against my thighs that i tasted of night

jasmine
and the earth after rain

do i taste of illness now of medications
acid and poison is my skin marked over
with toxic warnings no lover now could
know my body young or strong or healthy
no lover now could know the taste of me
before insulin before disease

is this still my body to give
and who would find this body beautiful
when i can't even
recognize it

ode to the syringe

o syringe   should i praise you   o syringe you must
know i am grateful   you have ensured   my life
continuing   you are a lasso a lariat a rope   a pair
of strong arms a tool for reining back the wild rebellions
of my blood

o syringe   i am your destiny   your function your
reluctant recipient o syringe   you are part   of my
story   part of my history   you like to follow my
relatives around   and around   and around

o syringe   sometimes you are effortless   o syringe
sometimes you deliver   a searing bundle of agony
that cannot be stopped   that can only be endured
sometimes you leave me wanting to scratch
under my skin

o syringe   how many of your kind have pierced my
skin   o syringe   i think more than two thousand
by now   and at the rate of four injections a day   the
numbers of your spent husks   are rapidly
accumulating

o syringe   i   should   praise   you

grace

another examining room. the young
physician's assistant walks in, greets me,
glances over my file puts everything
down. let's take a look at your feet to
start, she says. i bend down to take off my
shoes but she stops me, kneels down. I
apologize for not having had a pedicure,
for my unpainted toenails. she waves
away my apologies, and takes my right
foot in her hands and carefully removes
the shoe, then the sock. she holds my foot
carefully and asks me to close my eyes.

do you feel this, she asks, and this and this
and what about here and this. wonderful,
she says, you've lost no feeling at all. she
releases my right foot and lifts the left one
and treats it as gently and respectfully as
the first. I want to cry, I want to thank her
but I don't have the words. years of the
doctor turning away while I removed my
shoes. years of them wincing and trying
not to touch my skin with their gloved
hands, my still strong and sensitive feet
made ugly.

no one had ever treated my feet this way.
it was a gift to be seen as a person who'd
known joy and suffered pain, not the
automaton that doctors had poked and
prodded. doctors who never warned me
before they hurt me, who never even said

this might hurt. doctors who'd seen me at
my most vulnerable and had no human
look or touch or word they could spare
me.

I wanted to cry. this was a gift. as humble
and great a gift as if she had washed my
feet with her hair. this was a kind of grace.
my feet in her hands. how gently she put
my socks back on again, how she slipped
my shoes back on, how she too saw the
beauty of my simple feet.

en trozos/in pieces

i never met my mother's mother
concepción liguez lara died the year
      before i was born
my father told stories about rushing
her to the doctor to have her toe
her black fleshed toe amputated
my mother never said anything
      never said how she died
          never described her illness

the last time i saw my *tía* lupe
      it was my mother's funeral
my *tía* died two years later
i remember her strong graceful
lifting   herself out of the car into the wheelchair
      survivor of amputation toes feet legs
they'd begun on her fingers
      i remember her fierce expression

my father had been diabetic for six years
the only time i ever saw him cry
      was after the doctor told him
it was likely they would have to amputate his foot
he turned his face to the pillow
      body convulsing with broken sobs
he healed kept his feet for another eighteen years

after four years of silence i called
      when i heard he'd lost one foot
neither of us spoke of it
we spoke of living and of pain
      of dying and the end of fear
we said goodbye knew we would not speak again

later i learned they also amputated his other foot
            what he feared most was to go in pieces

                now i fear it too

strange dazed terror when i see the crutch
the walker the wheelchair the power scooters
terror when i see the missing foot the missing limb
strangers on the bus and at the store and at work
and on the street anywhere everywhere terror

yes limbs are lost everyday to war in car accidents
at work to freezing temperatures to violence
            but this is the terror of being devoured
one limb not being enough to satiate the beast
            this is the terror of going piece by piece

would i be strong enough
            to follow my *tía* lupe's example
would i want to could i see myself go in pieces
i think i would choose to live but i don't know
            there is a prayer i cannot help
diosito grant me 75 years of life to do my work
please i want to stay whole and strong
                able to walk

i know this is selfish
            i have already been given more than others
more life more strength more freedom more health
more love more time
            but i can't help wanting more
sometimes i hold my feet my calves in my hands
            stare at my fingers
i cannot comprehend my body without them

oh body *cuerpecito mio*

how many years i wasted not loving you
judging you for what they said you lacked
for what you were too much of
            too big too dark too fat too short too *india*
too masculine not pretty enough not feminine enough
not worthy of love
                  what does any of that matter now

oh body *cuerpecito mio*
            i will never see you through their eyes again
only through mine praising your strength
and your beauty the life i've lived through you
your joy and your endurance your hunger
            and your light
i will learn to take care of you
as i have learned to love you
no terror no terror
                  only love

iii. silence left and left the gate door open

one-sided conversations with my mother

cemetery

amá, when you were alive, i never once spoke to you in
english. now, ten years after your passing, i think there
are things i would like to say that i've never learned
how to say in spanish. for some conversations a
dictionary is a doorway. for others it is an obstacle.
                                        it's raining today
like it was the day you died. the way it rained in the
weeks after. someone said it meant the sky was
mourning with us, but i've always loved the rain. and so
did you. you rested when it rained. no fighting the sun's
heat. i imagine you could feel the hot earth sighing and
all the green leaves singing.

        your remains rest here. the earth is soft beneath
my feet. the grass springs back when i have passed. i
buried my braid here with you. you lay here alone, for
nine years minus one day, before they laid his remains
beside you. the ground above him seems fractured,
unsettled.

                            i am not the girl i was
ten years ago, amá. what would we say now
about death, about dying, about life.

kitchen

this is the kitchen where you made us meals without
number. i watched you so many times. the sink is
slightly rounded, here, where we both leaned against it
to wash dishes. this is the counter, with its speckled

yellow orange and green starburst pattern, where you made tortillas, where i laid out cookies, where we all always gathered.

it's been six years since moisés stood where you stood in this kitchen. washed chopped scraped peeled seasoned stirred kneaded tasted where you washed chopped scraped peeled seasoned stirred kneaded tasted.

i wept. he woke the walls the house the windows the floors. the air itself vibrated and shimmered remembering you. this was my home again. where you had been. i wept amidst the scent of onions and tomatoes simmering.

i would like to tell you about his *atole de avena,* the *arroz con leche,* his *carne guisada* made without flour, the dish he invented with *nopalitos.* how his cooking often made me want to cry. though he hardly spent any time in the kitchen with you, somehow he learned, like you, to infuse his cooking with love.

i never learned that. something always burns when i try. maybe if you explained it, i would understand.

so much i would like to tell you about my brother, your youngest son, the last gift you gave me.

garden

i remember you sneaking radishes as if they were a guilty pleasure. cucumbers by the double handful and fruit, always fruit. white grapes, red grapes, apples, oranges, bananas. a pan of sautéed spinach to ease your craving. *nopalitos* or green beans with a little onion and *chile. pan de elote* made without any flour.

46

you grew up close to the *monte,*
eating the land's bounty. you grew up with a
garden. i remember you poring over packs of seeds at
the store. how you longed to grow your own corn and
tomatoes and squash. you'd worked in fields all your
life, harvesting the food of others. but i knew what you
wanted. a little plot of land where you could watch your
own food grow from seed to leaf-ling to fruit-bearing plant.

apá's hunger
ruled the food we ate. he grew up on fried potatoes,
refried beans, fried meat. he only allowed iceberg
lettuce and tomatoes served at the table. i remember
one summer we ate fried chicken until the thought of it
made me want to vomit. i lived on biscuits and honey.

oh, the
conversations we could have now about growing food
and pesticides and nutrition and the benefits of fiber
and fresh produce and hormone-free meat and avoiding
preservatives and the causes of cancer.

oh, the causes of cancer.

hospice

i will always be grateful for this place. the kind and
graceful nurses. the blue serenity room. the separate
gathering area. the small moments of care. the visiting
harpist. the extra blankets. the couch where i slept. the
blooming plants outside the patio door. the vases of
fresh flowers volunteers brought.

they never said you had too many
visitors. and visitors came at all hours. a lovely place for
them to make their goodbyes. no cold and alien hospital.
the staff left us mostly alone that last morning. to hold

your hand as your breath slowed and everything but
your body fell away.

        we spent very little time speaking in your
last days. you spent a lot of time sleeping, especially
after they started the morphine drip. and then you
couldn't speak at all.

    so strange, you lying in silence.

           when i lived at home
after college, you never called or shook me awake. you
simply sat at the edge of my bed and started talking.
eventually, i'd respond. wake up. and our conversations
of the day would begin.

      i think we both chose our friends for their
ability to make interesting conversation. we delighted in
talking to strangers. people always said we looked alike
though our features were completely different. i
remember we were both so charmed when someone
said we had the same smile. do i resemble you more
now that i am older.

road

in my first memories of you, you are driving. dawn.
wind. the roar of the truck's engine. afternoon heat.
gritty dirt everywhere. dusk. a thousand miles of
highway unrolling before us.

    in my last memories of you, i drove your body
three hundred miles to its resting place. i didn't speak to
you then. everything in me was silent and still.

          so much we could say to
each other now. things i didn't know then. grief betrayal
pain illness. i would like to ask you about despair and
endurance. about the dimensions of the spirit. about

your memories. i want to hear you again telling me
every memory you shared and all the ones you didn't.
                    i'd have so much to tell
you about the last ten years. people i've met. things i've
done. who i am now.
                    i would like to share everything i've
learned about the indigenous identity you were never
ashamed of. i would read you poems, translating them
all. i would insist until you sang with me. i would have
so many questions.
            you'd be seventy-one now if you'd lived. if
you'd left apa all those years ago, we could have been a
happy little household of three. just you, me, and
moises. the three of us taking care of each other.
                        we could have been happy,
even with the other siblings coming in and out of our
lives. i don't know if you would have been able to resist
taking apá in when he was sick, when he was dying.
        i don't know.
                    your hair would be white now. it
had so little grey in it when the chemo and the radiation
took it all away. you would still have hardly any lines,
and no one would believe you were over seventy.
                    you and moisés
would have a garden. we'd repaint all the rooms in the
house. there would always be music. and laughing. we'd
all take forever to get up from the table after breakfast,
talking until our legs became restless. we'd take day
trips and road trips whenever we wanted, and drive as
slowly as we wanted. stopping whenever we wanted to
rest or take a look around. no hurrying. no leaving it till
next time.

waking

there is so much to say. so many stories to tell. your
absence lives in me.
there is no way to end this
conversation, amá. it has no end. it will never end...

susto

the old women say it is the accumulated weight
of so many *sustos* that cause diabetes
susto: not fright but trauma
and stress and shock and loss and grief
which *susto* do i blame for all this
which *susto* was the first to begin breaking down my resistance which
susto was the last straw
the knife that gutted me that drove me to the edge
pushed my body over which *susto* claimed victory and drove my very
cells to refuse the gifts of my blood
how do i name them all and
once named how do i uproot them unmake them and how do i heal

what's left behind

tequilita,

it's been five years, four months, three
days since you last touched my
lips. i remember that night. a
perfect night though there was no
singing. no *gritos* thrown against
the hot breeze.

you were the best tequila of my life.
smooth and fiery in a beautiful
bottle. my last tequila, you were a
gift from another writer. i didn't
know you'd be my last.

five years, four months, three days makes
it sound as if i were part of
alcoholics anonymous, but the
truth is— i left you for my liver. i
heard *pre-diabetic* and vowed
never again.

though from nineteen to twenty-eight, we
rampaged from one coast to
another, in south texas, on the
other side of the border, in austin
and san antonio. you made the
lights, the singing, the dancing all
the more beautiful. you were so
much a part of me, i even learned
to answer to your name.

but after that doctor's visit, i left you and
never looked back. i can't
understand those who can't live

without you and your kind. those
who take their pills with beer.
those who sit tranquil with a
pitcher of margaritas while their
blood burns.

for five years four months three days, i
have made the same choice. and
when i go to parties, i sip my *topo
chico* with lime, holding the bottle
by the neck, so i don't have to
explain *again* that i'm diabetic. or
listen *again* to all the people who
say, "but you can still drink—my
uncle, my mother, my cousin, my
friend, I—still drink
beer/wine/have a drink/take
shots and they're/I'm just fine."

i knew a young co-worker, diabetic at
twenty-one, who couldn't resist
her friends' calls for happy hours
and friday nights and saturday
nights and weekend games and
new year's eves.

she lived in and out of the hospital. i saw
her on new year's eve. she spent
the next six weeks fighting for her
life, for her kidneys,
because she wanted to celebrate
the new year like everyone else.

more than a decade ago i had a friend
        with type one diabetes who'd
        spent three weeks in a coma and
        woke suicidal. years passed. she
        liked to make margaritas by the
        pitcher. her two-year-old daughter
        knew how to dial 911.

another co-worker, years later, much
        younger and much thinner than
        me, wouldn't leave behind her
        drinking. it didn't take long. her
        hair started wisping away. she
        kept asking me "what am i doing
        wrong?" but she never listened.

never again, i said. i thank you, *tequilita,*
        for keeping your distance.
        whatever it may be that takes me, i
        know it won't be you.

neuropathy: poems of 4 words or less

my heart
breaks

        i remember you
            dancing

                  so much grace

you were so
strong

            we'd wander entire
              days

                      it began slowly

           it would get
              better

the dr said

                    it would get
                      better

your walk now
hesitant

the numbness spreading

                and sudden shooting pains

        torturous steps
          painfully balanced
                now i go alone

            all the time

you say it's spreading
         you tell me

        your body's
        growing quiet

                           i listen
                          am witness

but i don't know

          how it feels

             not to feel

lullaby

for my nieces and nephews

how do i tell you this gently how do i tell you this so that you hear it
like a lullaby it is a warning but i do not want to frighten you i do not
want to plant a seed of fear

how do i tell you i want to offer these words the way i would have
wanted to hear them given a choice i would have liked to hear them
until i understood until i believed

but like everyone else i never believed it would happen to me i thought
i had taken enough steps to protect myself i thought the odds were on
my side i thought i thought

but i didn't know as your parents do not know as your teachers do not
know as you do not know as your parents do not want to believe as
no one wants to believe

they will say you are too young to understand these things and you will
believe in the invincibility of your young bodies you do not really believe
you will age and grow old

even less would you believe someone telling you that with this family
history you are extremely at risk for cancer, heart disease, and yes,
diabetes and all its complications

it's not my imagination already you betray symptoms i do not want this
for you there are lessons i don't ever want to teach you advice i don't
ever want to give you

it does not matter that i changed your diapers and bought you toys and read you stories it does not matter that i was absurdly health absurdly strong until suddenly i wasn't

listen, learn everything you can choose always to live your lives with love there are no addictions worth the price of your dreams protect your bodies make them into fortresses

how do i tell you this gently how do i tell you this so that you hear it like a lullaby do not be afraid but make yourself strong be strong be strong and wake up wake up

wake up

soledad

(written with Moisés S. L. Lara)

whispering when he sings whispering we are the last memories before waking whispering when he sings when he sings no mourning did not come no we keep forgetting we will not remember there were ghosts here before death came there will be ghosts here after the living leave know that mourning did not come no no remembering no forgetting

silence came in the dark and stood in the morning light silence held the broken sounds silence shifted in its chair and silence made the beds silence ran outside embraced all the dead trees silence turned off the lights and told the walls to fall silence left and left the gate door open inviting in solitude there is no place where solitude has not entered

he woke so many times in the night never calling for anyone but with stories spilling out of him memories bruised from handling and memories never touched perfectly preserved and dangerous they left splinters they left glass they left spines they imploded and ate parts of his soul he woke so many times in the night and woke me so i could listen

there are words born of silence words born of violence others have always entrusted to me even before i knew what loss was they lived like blooms within and every new story is like rainfall fear of death fear of alone fear of being abandoned fear of pain others bring me their stories i could only bear them because i had song songs to make me strong

whispering when he sings whispering i always wanted to hear his voice singing he never understood what medicine it was never wondered what invites in the song what is the darkness descending inside and out how do you climb the song towards the light life sings life sings we keep forgetting we will not remember only the song remembers silence came in the dark and stood in the morning light silence held the broken sounds shadows don't sing shadows eat the silence and let it out again silence ran outside where there are no more gardens and the earth beckons with its stillness no rivers here silence left and left the gate door open there is no place where solitude has not been *iv.   i even speak light till the light subsides*

blood·sugar·*canto*

this is what they will not tell you
and this is what you must know
if you hear nothing else i say
hear this
you cannot live in fear
you cannot heal in fear
fear will never make you stronger

fear is the language many doctors speak
they'll say this is going to kill you
your organs are being bathed in acid
amputation dialysis coma death

and when the body does not obey
as the doctor demands
more pills
more insulin
more syringes
more often

and it will wear on you
the constant battle of
necessity versus necessity

a box of syringes
vs
gas money

the price of sufficient insulin
against
the cost of groceries

testing strips and lancets
vs
the light bill

the cost of one healthy meal
vs
the cost of three fast food meals

another co-pay
and another co-pay
vs
the cost of not seeing the doctor

they will say there are no choices
but there are always choices
though the choices
we make out of fear
are not choices

fear is a prison
fear is worse
than the disease
fear
takes
everything

some will say this is war
war raging within us
blood turned against itself
our bodies falling in battle
the enemy everywhere
within and without

but the word *war*
turns us against ourselves
and the word *disease*

renders us victims
and the war is unending
and a war always claims
casualties

in a war
there is no room
for dreaming oneself well
and the first part of the dream
is learning to listen
to *your body* and to *your blood*

it is not as simple
as
eat this not that eat that not this
take this not that take that not this
do this not that do that not this

you learn to listen
until you are the one writing the song
and the daily challenges
are the discordant notes
you must work into the score
making something more beautiful
than what there was before
not planned not wanted
but more powerful
because it is truth

but the music
will not come
if you are afraid
music like most things in life
enters in only one of two ways
el amor o el dolor

through love or through pain

i know
no one said
we were worthy of love
no one said
we were precious
or that our lives were gifts
no one said
let us learn to love ourselves
heal ourselves
care for ourselves
care for each other
teach each other
how to begin
with this essential task
of
loving ourselves

i will begin here
with these words
learning love
one utterance at a time

i will not
live
in fear

i will make song

the diabetic lover

it's not recommended,   my love
>   that i   cover your body   with whip crème
>   and chocolate syrup
>   maraschino cherries
>   for aesthetic emphasis

i could not dust you
>   with enough whey protein
>   to make up for all
>   those empty carbohydrates

>   i cannot tongue red wine
from your body
>   or drink shots
>   out of your navel
>   since that
>   would make me
>   quite literally
>   sick

but the thought of
>   grilled chicken breast
>   and veggies with half
>   a cup of brown rice
>   served on your skin
>   does not seem
>   conducive to
>   a night of passion

>   no   for sweetness
>   all i'd need would be

twenty five granules of
turbinado raw cane sugar
oh so carefully counted

one   on your left temple
that's where i'd begin
dark sweetness
exploding against my tongue
dark sweetness
in the scent of your hair

three on your tongue
while i pulled on your
lower lip with my teeth

one along your jaw
one down your neck and
one on your clavicle
i see sunlight and lush
green leaves playing
over your skin
two on one shoulder
and three trailing down
diagonally to your hip
i meant to use only my
lips mouth tongue
but my hands can't
resist following the
waves of your body
the ocean crashing
in my ears

i'd take five
in the palm of
my hand

and rasp them against
                           the tips of your
                 breasts
        drink in your gasp
                           then hunt for every bit
                                   of sugar cane dust
                                   while you sighed

                 three down
                           your abdomen
                 like far-flung
constellations

        my mouth
                 on your belly
                           always makes you
                                   curl up
                 i'd catch one foot
                           and then the other
                 place a granule
                                   on each arch

since raw cane sugar
                 doesn't dissolve at
                                   the first touch
                 i'd roll one granule
                           up your calf
                                   another from your
                                           knee to your thigh
one from your
                 thigh to your hip

and then i'd find
my twenty-five granules
gone

but no worries, my love
    i'd murmur against
        the apex of your thighs

            your sweetness
                always renders
    any   more
                excessive
                    and
                unnecessary

depression: an interrupted sestina

no one said the darkness only subsides
never disappearing   never dying
it is no ocean   it is no river
intermingling with my blood   it is my blood
my inheritance   my ancestral memory
my first word   my last   the words   in between

i eat   i sleep   i dream   i rage   between
fogs   i even speak light till the light subsides
a hundred songs to sing from memory
forgetting pain   forgetting all dying
i love   i give   i touch   i dance   my laughing blood
flowing in a bright burning river

but the next day   pours lies   pours filth   into the river
of my sleep   and there is a wall between
me and the world   the air tastes of blood
dust and rage   i don't remember what subsides
impossible to grasp   all the things that are dying
insisting insisting   abandon this memory

all lights
speak of stars
all stars
speak of living
but
all stars die

where
is
respite refuge rest
pain without end
hurting

71

outside myself
sinking
in through my skin

all stars
speak of silence
silence
sings the longest song
but all stars die

what is memory
to
this body
mothered
by
sadness

you don't know dying   you can't touch memory
listen to your whispering blood   find the river
breathe slowly in-between   wait till it subsides

shame: a ghazal in pieces

a body should have its wildness yes this body yes your body
who are they to name your body my body a shame body shame
my weight shame your weight shame how i look shame how
you look shame my disease shame my story say we have made
ourselves sick we keep ourselves sick what is the blame body
would it be easier if my body did not exist if your body did
not exist if all our diabetic bodies did not exist oh we will
not blame my body blame our bodies when my body has only
done everything it could to survive my body is a flame body
alive with fire fire pulsing inside shouting live live live my
story which is only triumphant because i am still here neither
pain nor shame will erase me or silence me there are poems
here too here in the places where all maps end your body
has survived my body has survived i will not be ashamed of
surviving

twosugars

.white.granulated.

soft sweet sand   crystal clouds   rasping on my skin   cold to
the touch   strange and hidden chemical scent   heavy
sweetness that won't stay   won't hold   it isn't real
remember being six   crying   a cherry lollipop in your mouth
        and making a hundred sugar cookies   bright lime
colored frosting   ama's oatmeal   the spoons of sugar melting
                        swirls of a woman's hair
blowing in the wind   fish with long feathery fins undulations
of sand dunes   and the drums   white ash   here bones here
desperation   and a word softer than pleasure   *poco veneno*
no mata   holly sugar   sugar beets my skin
                        doesn't want to eat this

.turbinado.raw.

dark and ripe woman-sweet sunlight swimming through green
leaves dark earth small intensities bursting   on the tongue
lingering cinnamon sand and the remnants of shells   the scent
lingers the taste lingers you can bite it
        we were walking in sugarcane fields   cutting the stalks
that first taste of green   sweet the tall green leaves swaying
in the wind   the blue sky   the birds swooping overhead
watching sticks being planted in the earth   one stick touching
the next stick   delight   rain on the window   dancing ladies
volcanoes the sound of rattlesnakes   rendered a whisper
drums more drums   pounding away in your blood   dancing
feathers
                        this is all you need

i call myself back

...every disease takes us in pieces in some way...cancer, ms, dementia, addiction, etc.
they all systematically rob us of ourselves. —Elizabeth Murphy

i call myself back from the pain from my horror
from my *susto* from all the moments i named
myself not normal sick diseased unable incapable
desperate despairing afraid crazed i call myself
back from nightmares from leg cramps from nausea
from forgetfulness from unconsciousness
and self-consciousness from waking fears from
loss from explanations i call myself back from the
nights i did not sleep from shed and unshed tears

i call us back from medication that hurts us as it
helps us from hospitals and pharmacies from
doctors and nurses from clinics and lab results
from blood draws and bandages from little books
with cramped numbers i call us back from
chemotherapy and radiation from dizziness from
neuropathy from side effects from exhaustion
i call us back from trembling limbs from more
prescriptions and more injections from everything
that removes us from natural medicine

but i will begin at the beginning reclamation
begins at every point i call myself back from
the child i was always alone afraid to be
abandoned unable to sleep i call myself back
from the child who was told she was ugly for
her dark skin and her round features i will

remember her as a child filled with the joy of
running child on a swing child on the roof
gazing at the sky and dreaming

i call us back from all our hurts here we all
are in our own pain our fear our shame our
guilt our anger i call us back from everything
that has taken us i call it all back our lands our
names our tongues our histories our stories
our gods our rivers our mountains our sacred places
our skies our stars i call us back from
everything that rendered us alien every time
we were told we did not belong every time we
were despised i call us back from poverty and
violence i take us back from malnutrition and
mis-education from war and from addiction i
call us back from silence and separation i call us back

we will not be robbed of ourselves not by
disease not by history not by the bureaucracies
of healthcare systems or governments not by
doctors who never listen not by a
socioeconomic order which prizes cultural
erasure not by drug companies who do not
believe our pockets are finite not by the
capitalist system that extracts our labor until it
abandons us like broken machinery we call
ourselves back we call ourselves back

we have walked through fire through burning
infernos we have wept we have suffered
we call ourselves back we have survived we

have become stronger we call ourselves back
we have not lost any part of ourselves we are
not diminished we call ourselves back
we are whole.

v.   let my last breath be song

the world is medicine

let it in
the sunshine the rain the wind the lightning
                eat the raw
                eat the stones and eat the marrow
                      eat the warmth on your skin
                and the words the sun is writing
        eat the scent of the earth after rain
        eat the storm the thunder rumbling inside

this is how you grow strong
be the roar be the keening
      be the screaming be the running
      be louder
              be the wind be the trees growing tall
              be the word be the day be the knife
be the hot rush of blood
be the clouds
                be the electric spill of blooming
                flowers in the desert

begin
and end with water
        never forget
        the ocean lives inside us
              the rivers take us
              where our ancestors
          walked
      our bodies still ebb and flow
      with the tides
              there is no joy like the joy of the body
              suspended in water weightless and fierce
water is life
drink it in

touch the world eat the world be the world
the world is medicine

    let
    it in

when wind blows through them

i. world

i see them sometimes
sometimes
i hear them
all the birds inside you
a thousand feathered shades
of every color
fluttering inside you
and all the
cooing whistling warbling
singing humming hooting
chirping cawing calling
they were drawn
to the haven
inside you
where nature itself
takes refuge
daily you cultivate
an entire interior world
and all the leaves and blossoms
of the world have come
to you
before they disappear
from the outside world
poor and polluted
and here you nurse them
bless them cleanse them

find them sun and shade
a place in your fertile
soil
waterfalls inside you
and at dawn
the sky is pink

ii. spider

i lost my breath
when i heard her say
the spider is my mother
i thought
she must know
lovepainmemory's
dimensions
know them
without words
in silence
know them
with her hands
spanning
the distance between ear
and the tip of her nose
she shares
our language

in your name
i would erect massive
monuments
of wrung glass
glass the color of sky
one massive breath
of your creating

84

thunder lightning wind and rain
in your infinite embrace

iii. refuge

you are silence
and the thrumming
of a thousand hearts
you are what
i have learned of
forgiving
healing
evolving
remembering

you are stronger
than i will ever be
wringing beauty
and creation
out of pain and loneliness

tenderness for
green life and small creatures
pouring from your scarred hands

forgiving hurt
and the memory of hurt

the world sings in you
skyspider
brotherspider

and
like
a
hummingbird
i
take refuge
in you

love song for my organs

this is a song i didn't know
needed singing needed singing

a song for each morning
a song for each night

offered with awareness
offered with gratitude

decades have passed i did not
know your colors your shapes

the work you do have done
or what you needed from me

now i know this song needs singing
i will sing it everywhere i go

i name you now breathe softly
upon you hold you tenderly within

kidneys

you are not forgotten never
you are cherished and i am grateful

i bring you rainwater and riverwater
i bring you flowers tiny blue flowers

i bring you these my two hands filled
with sun light with starlight

i sing you strong sing you whole
and thank you for filtering my blood

heart

be strong little heart as strong as you
have ever been you are my life

when i am still i hear your beating
feel it in my chest hold you close

in a dance that will not pause while
we are living i envision the flow of blood

flowing to you flowing from you moving easily
moving swiftly through wide open blood vessels

pancreas

you have been sleeping little warrior
it is time to wake time to speak again

i will bring you morning serenades
cascading flower petals and trilling birdsong

you fought the rising glucose hordes fought
until you were spent until you could not go on

years now i have lived on foreign insulin
always approximate subject to wild swings

of not enough too much almost in time
i long for your fine tuned calibration

i see you rising i hear you murmuring
words spoken at dawn i greet you

liver

lean i dream you lean see you lean and dark
brow furrowed ferociously inspired sculptor

ferociously creating ferociously shaping each
work of art as if it were the first time the only time

as if you were recreating the ocean the stars every minute
you are not a factory not an assembly line

i bring you milk thistle i bring you flax seed in thanks
you are re-creating my life your art is my life

nerves

you tell me stories without you there are no stories
without them i would know nothing understand nothing

of the world within or the world without
you are the carriers of lightning of moonlight

you tell me i am alive you tell me i am safe
because of you the exquisite the tender of my life

and also the pain and also the hurt the sharp the ache
but tell me stories i will always be listening

skin

hot breath tender touch running bare-fleshed in the rain
the warmth of the sun the chill of winter days the wind

my boundaries my beginnings my endings my whole

life the whole world written on my skin my skin sings

i will bring you gifts in thanks jojoba aloe avocado sweet
almond oil cocoa butter calendula shea butter and lanolin

eyes

for me everything begins with you I could spend days staring
at the sky day or night or morning or fog or thunderstorm

so much sweetness in looking at green leaves bright colors
loved faces blossoms rivers rainfall sunshine long roads

in my memories everything begins with what you've given me
i remember my life in a million images you brought me

and all the words of my life all the books of my life
for all the flames and the moonlight all my gratitude

gratitude

kidneys....heart....pancreas....nerves
liver....skin....eyes....all my body

please forgive any harm
i have caused you

thank you for this day for
every day you have given me

now i know this song needs singing
i will sing it everywhere i go

i name you now breathe softly
upon you hold you tenderly within

dreaming in blossom

so many times i saw you bend down to smell a flower your eyes closed
your forehead smooth your body suspended in
                                        anticipation
at first the first years you lived with me
                                    i'd always laugh in delight seeing
you this way like an ecstatic ruby throated hummingbird
                                        i always loved taking
you to gardens to plant nurseries loved to see you with books on
flowers reading about flowers
                        telling me about flowers because of you i learned
their names
            stargazer lilies and cyclamens and ixora hyacinths hydrangeas
irises birds of paradise peonies calla lilies
                                how many times did i ask you
their names and you were always patient
                                marigolds petunias daisies African
violets begonias lantana azaleas poppies Carolina Jessamine wisteria
                                                you named
them every time we drove past them like incantations like poetry
                                    you never tired of hearing
a poetry that fed your soul it fed mine too
                                paintbrush nightshade rain lilies yucca
pink primrose mountain laurel winecups
                                decades with you were not enough
i miss you every day wish i could speak to you every day
                                        forgive me i'd want to say
forgive me for never bringing you enough flowers
                                    forgive me for the time it took
me to find us a house and build you a sunroom
                            forgive me for all the times i didn't listen
                            forgive me for all the times i hurt you

and i'd want to ask you
           did you know you were the blossom of my life
                        the sweetness of my life
so fierce and truthful you were so brilliant
                to talk with you was to touch iridescence
thank you i'd want to say i never said it enough thank you thank you
thank you
you made me stronger than i was you still make me stronger than i am
                      you taught me
the language of orchids of epiphytes phalaenopsis cattleya vanilla
epidendrum dendrobium
      and the patience of flower spikes their careful buds and their
long-lived leaves
           i speak to you all the time waking and sleeping
                          i think of you
every time i see a flower blooming any of a thousand colors
                  you speak to me in blossoms
                  you speak to me in sunshine
i am never alone you are with me always
                infinite and leafing
                  blossoming

neuropathy #2

in the   sun   shining bright warmth
    he says
          light, it is us

huisache seedlings   gently touched   caressed   verdant whisperings
    can he feel them?
      he says   without being asked   without question
the sunlight within hears heartbeats he feels intention growth
breath
their scent
    he says
         remind him of newborns
               to him, to me
                   they are his children

held   he holds me   embraced   with his arms entirely
       such long arms, big hands
            holds me so close   i can barely hear him
                         breathing
           he pats me   calls me puppy we laugh because
i can't see his face   i can't   see his face
               but he makes me laugh
                but he is trying
                  not to cry
in his gaze with out   side   without
    his knowing
       a single tear
      falls
        from his eye, slowly
   the wind has been constant   the wind in his gaze
       a wind   that winds and springs that coils that
preens

he says
    is the wind blowing?
        yes,
           i
             say

there will be singing in the morning

and singing in the night singing in the days
of want and singing in the days of plenty
singing alone and singing with ghosts
singing old songs and singing new songs we
will remember songs we haven't heard yet
songs that haven't been dreamt yet songs no
one has found the words for songs sung on
the road and songs sung in bed songs sung
while weeping and songs sung while waiting
songs for breath and sun and light and
moon and earth and water songs for
sustenance we will sing impossible songs
indecipherable songs songs that cannot be
heard and songs that cannot be shared
we will sing songs without words silent songs
and screaming songs songs that tremble and
songs we can embrace
                         song and i live in
each other's skins song and i breathe each
other's breath take refuge in each other
passing silver fire light between each other's
lips hot and cold at once naming and un-
naming freeing ourselves taking wing song
and i spiraling in the sky i would like to die
singing let there be song in my throat
spilling out let my last breath be song

Acknowledgments

my gratitude to Moisés S. L. Lara for the amazing cover artwork, for many conversations and much inspiration, and for a great deal of the editing...

my thanks to Diana Marie Delgado, Brandon Shuler, and Jo Reyes-Boitel for early criticism...

a great big thank you to CantoMundo for making me remember that I will always be a poet...

profound thanks to Ruth Thompson, Don Mitchell, and Saddle Road Press for giving these poems a home...

mil gracias to Demetria Martínez, Tim Z. Hernandez, Willie Perdomo, and Barbara Jane Reyes for their beautiful blurbs...

my thanks to the Alfredo Cisneros del Moral Foundation for support and time to work on final revisions...

and my appreciation for the following publications that first published the following poems:

"love song for my organs" and "ode to the syringe" in *Huizache*; "shame: a ghazal in pieces," "you do not listen," and "two sugars" in *La Tolteca Zine*; "en trozos/in pieces" and "one-sided conversations with my mother" in *Entre Guadalupe y La Malinche Anthology*; "blood-sugar-canto," "dieta indigena," and "the world is medicine" in *El Mundo Zurdo 4 Anthology*; "one-sided conversations with my mother" in *La Palabra-The Word is a Woman/Mothers and Daughters Anthology*; "en trozos/in pieces" in *Luna Luna Magazine*; "despair" in the *2014 AIPF Anthology*; "neuropathy: poems of 4 words or less" in *Mujeres de Maiz*; excerpts from "love song for my organs" in *ToeGood Poetry*; "the diabetic lover" in *GRITS Anthology*; "i call myself back" in *Chicana/Latina studies—MALCS Journal*; "diabetic love song" in *AS/US*; "labwork," "depression: an interrupted sestina," and "the world is medicine" in *Clackamas Literary Review*; "*dieta indigena*" in *KUIKATL*; "song for fear" in *Generations*; "there will be singing" in *Rabbit and Rose*; "when the wind blows through them" and "dreaming in blossom" in *Ginosko Literary Review*; "diabetic epidemic" in *Gulf Stream Anthology*; "we don't give morphine for heartburn" in *Mas Tequila Review*; "poem to frida, patron saint of art and pain" in *BorderSenses*; "*soledad*" in *Palabra*; "*susto*" in *El Retorno*.

The following poems were also published in a bilingual digital chapbook (Sibling Rivalry Press, 2015): "april 23, 2008"; "*en trozos*/in pieces"; "one-sided conversations with my mother"; "*tequilita*"; "lullaby"; "diabetic epidemic"; "*susto*."

About the Author

ire'ne lara silva lives in Austin, TX, and is the author of *furia* (poetry, Mouthfeel Press, 2010) which received an Honorable Mention for the 2011 International Latino Book Award and *flesh to bone* (short stories, Aunt Lute Books, 2013) which won the 2013 Premio Aztlan, placed 2nd for the 2014 NACCS Tejas Foco Award for Fiction, and was a finalist for *Foreward Review*'s Book of the Year Award in Multicultural Fiction.

ire'ne is the recipient of the 2014 Alfredo Cisneros del Moral Award, the Fiction Finalist for AROHO's 2013 Gift of Freedom Award, and the 2008 recipient of the Gloria Anzaldua Milagro Award, as well as a Macondo Workshop member and CantoMundo Inaugural Fellow. She and Moisés S. L. Lara are currently co-coordinators for the Flor De Nopal Literary Festival.

Printed in the USA
CPSIA information can be obtained
at www.ICGtesting.com
LVHW041335021223
765434LV00005B/660